TO DR. JACK[...]

WITH THANKS FOR VISITING [...] +

LOOKING FORWARD TO YOUR RETURN!

BEST WISHES,

NOVARTIS

(ARABIAN GULF)

The UAE
Formative Years
1965 - 75

MOTIVATE
PUBLISHING

The UAE
Formative Years
1965 - 75

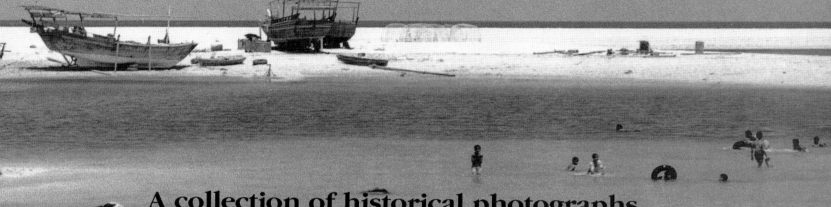

**A collection of historical photographs
by Ramesh Shukla**

Written by Asha Bhatia

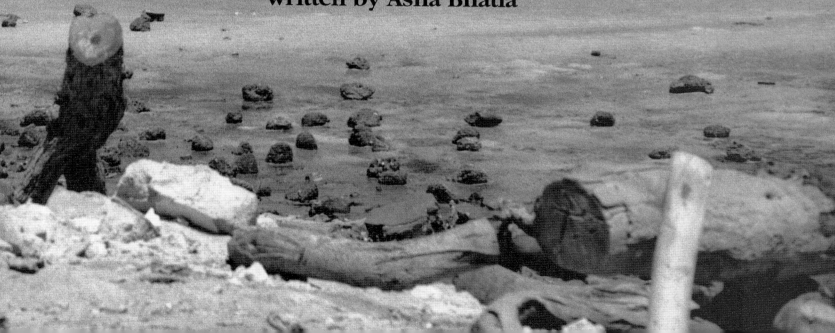

Published by Motivate Publishing

Dubai: PO Box 2331, Dubai, UAE
Abu Dhabi: PO Box 43072, Abu Dhabi, UAE
London: London House, 19 Old Court Place,
Kensington High Street, London W8 4PL

Directors:
Obaid Humaid Al Tayer
Ian Fairservice

First Published 1995

© Ramesh Shukla and Motivate Publishing 1995

ISBN: 1 873544 70 7

British Library Cataloguing-in-Publication Data.
A catalogue record for this book is available from the British Library.

Printed by Emirates Printing Press, Dubai.

Foreword

Ramesh Shukla's photographs, some of which have been exhibited on a number of occasions, form an invaluable record of the recent history and development of the United Arab Emirates, and now, in this book, can be seen and appreciated by a wider audience.

Residents of the UAE have experienced more change in the past 30 years than those of perhaps any other country. While it is right that both nation and individuals should look to the future, it is also important, particularly for the younger generation, to retain a sense of heritage – for we are all shaped by our past. Quiet pride should be taken in the enormous progress that has been achieved, the benefits this has brought and the sure foundations that have been laid for future prosperity.

Three decades ago it would have been difficult to envisage the local production of a book such as this – or, indeed, to imagine that there would be a population sufficiently large to make it worthwhile. That, in its own way, is a measure of the development that has taken place since Ramesh Shukla first started recording the world seen in these pages.

Motivate Publishing
December 1995

Contents

Introduction

The Sheikhdoms that joined together to form the United Arab Emirates were formerly independent sovereign states, six – Abu Dhabi, Dubai, Sharjah, Ajman, Umm Al Quwain and Ras Al Khaimah – scattered along the southern coast of the Arabian Gulf between Qatar and Oman, and the seventh – Fujairah – facing the Arabian Sea. Britain, with whom the states of the lower Gulf had long been under treaty, had announced in 1968 that it would withdraw from the area in three years' time, leaving the Sheikhdoms a stark choice: either they must succeed in the difficult (and considered by many to be the impossible) task of forging a nation from these fiercely independent components or they would, in all probability, disintegrate in a maelstrom of petty boundary squabbles and disagreements.

The odds against the formation, let alone the maintenance, of a successful union of the Trucial States (as they had been known for more than a century) appeared great and the world watched with some cynicism when the first moves towards establishing a federation were initiated just weeks after the British Government's announcement. Not only did Britain's withdrawal end the treaty-bound protection from external aggression provided to the Sheikhdoms, but they would now also need to establish joint control over economic development, foreign affairs and internal security – impossible without the creation of a full governmental infrastructure. With their small populations and then unexploited natural resources the survival of a united nation seemed doubtful.

However, two personalities emerged whose towering presence bound the first slender threads of national unity together: His Highness Sheikh Zayed bin Sultan Al Nahyan, Ruler of Abu Dhabi, a decisive, benevolent and fatherly figure, and His Highness Sheikh Rashid bin Saeed Al Maktoum, Ruler of Dubai, who combined extraordinary business acumen with the foresight of a visionary. These allies were both determined to create a nation which would develop and prosper.

On February 18, 1968, at the small village of As-Sameeh in the emirate of Abu Dhabi, the two Rulers discussed the future – and at this meeting they resolved to unite their two emirates. The agreement they signed spelt out the reason for their historic decision, stating that they were federating out of their "desire to preserve stability" in their states and "to realise a better future" for their people. The agreement specified foreign affairs, security, defence, social services and immigration as subjects that would be within the domain of federal authorities. Simultaneously the Rulers of Sharjah, Ajman, Umm Al Quwain, Ras Al Khaimah, Fujairah, Qatar and Bahrain were invited to join them.

A prompt response to the invitation was received from the other seven Rulers, who were also considering a similar common agenda. As a result, all nine met in Dubai on February 27, just nine days after the crucial Zayed/Rashid meeting at As-Sameeh. The agreement signed that day was based on the Abu Dhabi/Dubai pact, and stated that the formation of a federation to include all the emirates in the Gulf "is more satisfactory for the realisation of the purposes of these two emirates and is wanted by the people of the area".

The agreement highlighted the reasons for the formation of the federation, foremost amongst which was the need to support the strong fraternal bonds amongst the emirates. A federation, it reiterated, would enable the different countries to work together for their own good as well as for the benefit and well-being of all Arab peoples. Furthermore it would help ensure the internal stability of all the Sheikhdoms and permit them to create a common means of defence.

The Dubai meeting also established a Supreme Council made up of the Rulers of the nine states. Charged with drawing up a charter for the federation and formulating policies on both internal and external matters, the Council met many times during 1969 and 1970 but was unable to reach a mutually satisfactory agreement on the creation of a single, cohesive state. The Deputy Rulers were set the task of redrafting the constitution in

order to accommodate the differing points of view, but success eluded them and Bahrain and Qatar eventually elected to work towards separate independence outside the framework of the proposed federation.

Far from being disillusioned the other seven emirates – spurred on by the determination of Sheikh Zayed and the enthusiasm of Sheikh Rashid – worked even harder towards achieving a solution. Abu Dhabi in particular pursued the quest for unity by offering to federate with any or all of the emirates, a proposal that was taken up by each of the emirates that now comprise the UAE, with the exception of Ras Al Khaimah. At a meeting of the Rulers, held in Dubai on July 18, 1971, the constitution that had formerly been proposed was endorsed as the provisional constitution for the new country – and the decision was taken to form the United Arab Emirates on December 2 of that year. Whilst in the meantime Bahrain and Qatar had become independent states, on February 10, 1972 Ras Al Khaimah, having overcome its reservations over some aspects regarding representation, decided to join the UAE.

At the meeting on that hot July day in 1971 Sheikh Zayed was elected President of the UAE and Sheikh Rashid Vice-President. A fitting tribute to the two leaders whose initiative, vigour and resolution had forged a nation from the disparate and autonomous Sheikhdoms – a nation that has grown and prospered as they had planned.

1965

The divers who searched for pearls on the sandy seabed off Abu Dhabi in the early years of the twentieth century would have been unable even to imagine the vast wealth that lay beneath the sea. Whilst the pearls they found had given the emirate its early riches, deeper, much deeper, was an abundance of resources that would transform the land and its peoples in a manner and at a pace unparalleled anywhere in the world.

Initial explorations were hardly auspicious. In 1950 the first well, Murban 1, delivered very little and Murban 2, in 1958, struck only gas – although that was an indication of the presence of oil reserves. Murban 3 was the first strike in Abu Dhabi to produce 5,000 barrels a day but it was not until 1962, after more wells had been drilled, that it was recognised that the emirate's future was promising indeed. Abu Dhabi Marine Areas (ADMA) Ltd – jointly formed by British Petroleum and Compagnie Française des Pétroles – was granted concessions to explore offshore over an area of 20,000 square kilometres. By the end of 1962 ADMA was exporting 800,000 tonnes per year – and by 1965 an annual total of four million tonnes. But even that total was to be dwarfed by the find at Zakhum, 90 kilometres from Das Island, the annual output of which had reached 20.7 million tonnes by 1972.

In Dubai oil had yet to be discovered and the city's future then, as now, was seen to be in trade. In 1958 Sheikh Rashid had approached the Government of Kuwait and secured a loan of $960,000 for the purpose of dredging the creek and constructing a breakwater at its entrance to stop the formation of sand-bars. After completion of the first phase in 1963 the creek was then further deepened and a mile-long steel-piled wharf was built, encouraging more dhows – and even larger vessels – to call at Dubai. By this time a small airstrip had also been completed which further enhanced facilities for trading, especially in gold which was flown in from Zurich, Geneva and London to be loaded on dhows bound for India.

But even earlier than this Dubai had taken the first tentative step towards developing a modern infrastructure by the introduction, in 1952, of electricity and the telephone – the former in the shape of 23 lamp-posts at the abra point. By 1957 Dubai Municipality was entrusted with such varied responsibilities as setting up and running hospitals, the fire brigade and markets. And in 1965 the Dubai Chamber of Commerce, the first to be established in the Trucial States, was given wide-ranging responsibilities in regulating trade and advising the government on commercial legislation. Drawn from Dubai's cosmopolitan business community the Chamber was administered by a nine-member committee which comprised Juma Al Majid, Sultan Ali Al Owais, Seif Ahmed Al Ghurair, Majid Mohammed Al Futtaim, Mohammed Saeed Al Mulla, Mohammed Abdulla Al Kaz, Mohammed Hadi Badri, Hashem Khoory and Maghanmal Jethanand.

The first meeting was held in the office of Majid Mohammed Al Futtaim to elect from amongst themselves five office-bearers. Sheikh Rashid then provided a grant of Rs 50,000 and an office in Nasser Square from which the Chamber began its activities. Amongst the first pieces of legislation discussed by the Chamber was a draft law calling for the immediate arrest of anybody issuing a cheque which was subsequently dishonoured due to insufficient funds. Still in force today, the law has made a significant contribution to the disciplined trade practices of the emirate.

In Sharjah the region's first school opened in 1953 providing structured education for some 450 male students aged between six and seventeen years. Until that time rudimentary schooling had been provided by Qur'anic teaching at madrassahs attached to community mosques, but so successful was the new facility that other emirates, acknowledging the importance of education, built their own schools.

◀ *Dubai's creek has played a pivotal role in the history of the emirate, the natural anchorage providing a rare haven on the important trade routes that ran through the Gulf, linking Europe and the Far East. Although there had been a small town here for some considerable time, in 1833 a branch of the Bani Yas from Liwa settled in Dubai – and it was one of the leading families from this group, the Maktoums, that were to develop the infant city into the region's leading commercial centre.*

At high tide, before the creek was dredged and reclamation took place on Deira-side, the water lapped the walls of the buildings – whilst at low tide it was often possible to walk across the creek with the help of a bridge formed by moored abras in the deeper central channel. Ramesh remembers helping to place boulders and assisting in fixing mooring posts.

The foreground of this photograph is where Bani Yas Street, between the Sheraton and Inter-Continental hotels, stands today. The silhouetted skyline of Bur Dubai includes the British Embassy, where the last Political Agent, David Roberts, lived. The high water tank and solitary boat are long gone but, as Ramesh observed, whilst many things have changed in Dubai, the beauty of the sunsets remain.

▲ It is Juma – Friday, the day of prayer and rest in the Islamic world – providing an opportunity for this group of ladies, gathering close to where the Hyatt Regency now stands, to relax in the winter sunshine and discuss children, meet friends and exchange news.

◄ A heritage in stone, the windtowers of Bastakia were built to capture any passing breeze and send its cooling draughts down into the interior of the house. Four-sided, the towers would catch the wind from any direction – and the taller they were the more efficiently they functioned. The attractive, decorative plaster-work panels were a means of ventilating the house without losing privacy – combining aesthetic appeal with practicality. Incorporating elements of traditional Islamic design, no two are identical yet each contributes to a sense of uniformity in the building as a whole. The projecting wooden poles, chandals, often served as ready-made scaffolding for maintenance.

▲ Sharjah Corniche, now lined with elegant palaces and five-star hotels, presented a less developed aspect in 1965. Silt had reduced the depth of Sharjah's creek so that at some points even small dhows were unable to use it and many ships were forced to find other ports of call.

▶ A mid-day snooze on board a dhow moored at the jetty in Abu Dhabi – a scene that can still be observed today at harbours around the country. This photograph was so appreciated by a European visitor in 1975 that he purchased 2,000 copies.

▲ *During Eid festivities the Razfa, a traditional dance that is both a celebration and a greeting, is performed — sometimes for visiting dignitaries but more often than not just as a spontaneous expression of pleasure. During the dance sequence two groups of men weave back and forth, in turn chanting lines of a folk song. Most songs are rooted in the poetry of the region, which — whilst noted for its clever phraseology and its double entendres — also often provides a living record of a particular tribe's history, its triumphs and tribulations, love stories and exploits.*

This celebration took place at Al Ain and provided entertainment for a group of Pathan labourers from Afghanistan and Pakistan, suitably attired in their traditional headgear.

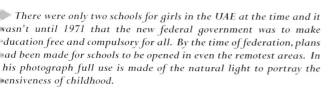
The Old Fort at Al Ain now forms part of a museum complex. Nowadays reached easily by modern highways, in 1965 travellers from Dubai had to journey over rudimentary roads via Abu Dhabi, showing their passports at the border and obtaining clearance through checkpoints. Ramesh recalls the hospitality of the officials who would offer gahwa – Arabic coffee, and sulaimani – a local tea.

There were only two schools for girls in the UAE at the time and it wasn't until 1971 that the new federal government was to make education free and compulsory for all. By the time of federation, plans had been made for schools to be opened in even the remotest areas. In this photograph full use is made of the natural light to portray the pensiveness of childhood.

Although appointed Governor of Al Ain in 1946 by his brother, Sheikh Shakhbut, it was not until twenty years later that Sheikh Zayed bin Sultan Al Nahyan became Ruler of Abu Dhabi – an important milestone on his long career as a leader which would culminate in his Presidency of the United Arab Emirates.

In 1966 oil was struck some 90 kilometres offshore to the south-west of Dubai in what was later named the Fateh field, and three years later the emirate joined the ranks of the world's oil producers, albeit on a modest scale. Whilst the discovery of oil did not make as great an impact on Dubai's economy as had been the case with other Gulf states – the city's prosperity was already firmly based on trade – the revenues enabled the rapid development of the creek, Port Rashid and other major projects, turning the city into one of the boom areas of the Middle East.

In the same year the rules of the Dubai Department of Customs, formed in 1962, were updated and rewritten by Bill Duff, a financial expert who had come to Dubai from Kuwait. The regulations he drew up, formalised into a legal format by Adi Bitar, became the 1966 Customs Ordinance which several other Gulf states were to use as a model.

Many of Dubai's economic and political achievements were recorded on postage stamps of the time. Between 1963 and 1972 the Dubai Government issued more than 400 different stamps over 63 issues, marking such varied events as the opening of the city's first automatic telephone exchange (on January 14, 1966) and the Gulf Arab summit conference of the same year – commemorated by a remarkable set of horizontal stamps showing the portraits of the seven Rulers of the Trucial States and the Emirs of Bahrain and Qatar.

Values on Dubai stamps were shown in the Indian currency of naye paise and rupees until, in 1966, the Qatar-Dubai riyal was introduced. The first issue to show the new currency – which remained in use until the establishment of the UAE dirham – was the World Cup football championship series of October 1, 1966.

Between Fujairah and Ajman, in a simple dressing room created below the branches of a tree next to a barasti hut, a lady ties her burqa in the light of a kerosene lamp. In those days cameras were rare in the emirates, and quite possibly the lady was completely unaware of being photographed.

▲ Immigration formalities in 1966 were carried out by an official who checked papers alongside the dhows. As the vessels could not come close to the bank, where the water was too shallow, wooden quays were constructed – from which a precarious climb along a plank was the only way to board for these passengers bound for the subcontinent.

◀ Although the banks of Dubai creek are now lined with elegant buildings and parks, the location shown in this photograph, taken from Shindaga and looking across the curve of the creek to Al Ras, is still immediately recognisable today. The vessels in the foreground are standing on the silted bottom of the creek, still not dredged at this point.

Less easily recognisable thirty years on is Abu Dhabi's Corniche. The town, from which the emirate takes its name, is so called because of a hunting trip undertaken by Sheikh Dhiyab bin Isa of the Manasir tribe, in 1761. Having travelled from Liwa, part of his group pursued a gazelle which led them over to the island on which the city now stands, where they found a fresh water spring. On being informed of this Sheikh Dhiyab decreed that the place should be known as Abu Dhabi – the father or homeland of the gazelle.

▲ *A plume of flying sand was evidence that people were returning along the track to Sharjah after a day's business in Dubai. Whilst camels could make the trip relatively easily – if somewhat slowly – vehicle traffic was restricted to four-wheel drives. The tracks to Abu Dhabi or Ras Al Khaimah ran alongside the water's edge and would often flood at high tide, rendering them impassable even to four-wheel-drive vehicles. A good driver on a good day would still take four hours to reach Abu Dhabi from Dubai. Work on developing inter-state roads began in 1967, the Dubai-Sharjah connection being the first.*

▼ *Despite its connection with the ruling family, the building on the right of this picture is referred to not as a palace but simply as Sheikh Saeed's house. The former residence of Sheikh Rashid, son of Sheikh Saeed — he was born and brought up here — its majlis was an important part of Dubai's administration until 1958 when the new Zabeel Palace was built.*

The large vessel, proudly flying the Dubai flag, is entering the creek to unload a mixed cargo of cows, calves, onions and potatoes.

The aromatic scents of the Spice Souq in Deira made it a good place to conduct meetings, drink tea, reconcile accounts and generally chat about business and the economy. The original structure was built of wood and stood at the edge of the creek.

When Ramesh first came to Dubai he set up home and studio in a
spacious villa close to Nasser square, where the Al Manal Centre and
Pic 'n' Save supermarket now stand. Even then it was a busy area, the
house being adjacent to the livestock market where the trading of
goats and camels continued from dawn to dusk. Here on a misty
morning a water-seller carries his cans — a heavy load judging by the
curve in the wooden pole.

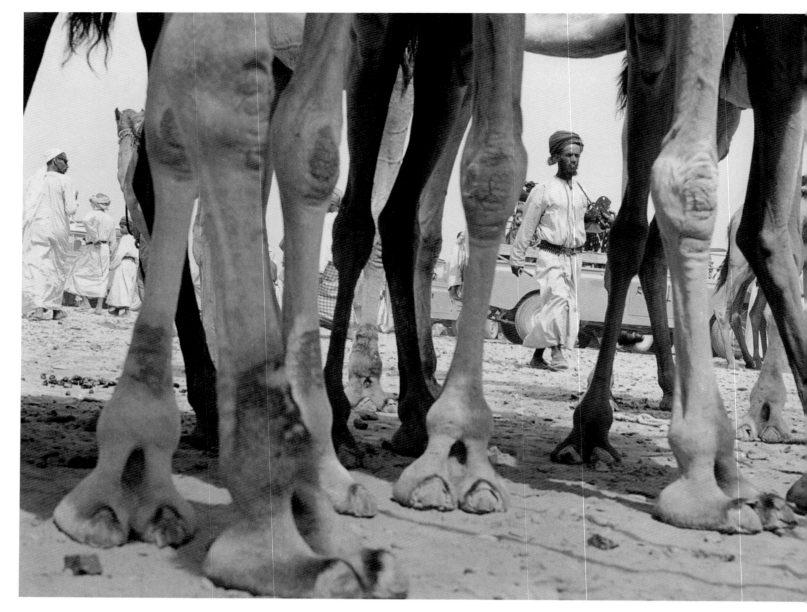

▲ *An Omani gentleman is seen through the legs of a group of camels at Deira's market. During long journeys across the desert when drinking water was not available, fresh milk from the camel, containing vitamin C and salt, was an important element of the Bedu diet.*

▶ *A man stands by a flagpole as a group of ladies in Fujairah gather for a wedding celebration. Even when dressed in their finery they still had to contend with the elements — and the sand: not easy on what was evidently a windy day.*

Many women still wore the veil in public but throughout the emirates significant social changes were taking place. As early as 1967 women were employed in radio and television – the first female broadcaster coming from Sharjah and working at the radio station established in 1967 by the Trucial Oman Scouts – and since that time the Ministry of Information and Culture has encouraged the employment of women as broadcasters.

Abu Dhabi joined OPEC in 1967, seven years after the organisation had been formed. Oil and gas had given the citizens a way of life undreamed of just a few years before and the income was being used to bring about changes that reached every aspect of life in both the cities and remote villages. An early priority was the establishment of schools for children of all ages – the Rulers appreciating the importance of a well-educated population if the country was to develop its full potential – and facilities were rapidly expanded. In Dubai the English Speaking School had just 50 pupils, amongst whom was the daughter of the Political Agent, David Roberts.

Although work on the first town roads in Dubai, around the Gold Souq, had commenced only in 1964 – and had been the cause of some excitement since before then there was little point in owning a conventional two-wheel-drive car – in 1967 the tarmac road linking Dubai and Sharjah was under construction. Until then travel between the emirates had been a lengthy process – David Roberts recalled spending six hours in a Land Rover driving across the desert to see the Ruler of Fujairah. But despite the lack of many facilities now taken for granted, the community was a happy one made up then, as now, of hard working people of all races, creeds and nationalities.

In those pre-oil days, Dubai was already thriving, its creek filled with vessels and its merchants prospering. But even greater change was coming, foreshadowed by the sight of the first oil platform, the huge structure towering over the little town as it was towed out of the creek to sea.

◄ *The sabka market in Deira Souq had no permanent structure, the shops being made from plywood and the goods – vegetables, fruit, clothes, books and a hundred other items – being sold from cardboard cartons. It was a busy market even then and, just as today, bargaining for the right price was both accepted and respected.*

▲ On this ornate balcony in Bastakia the design motifs are in pairs — but not identical since the work was carried out by hand. Note the two coffee pots rising elegantly above the balustrade.

▶ In a relaxed mood and with his pipe beside him, Sheikh Rashid sip a cup of sulaimani tea. Serving sulaimani tea and gahwa coffee is long-standing custom in the UAE.

Freshly ground gahwa coffee is flavoured with cardamom an poured from the traditional long-spouted dolla seen here. It is polit to accept up to three cups but when the visitor has had enough the cu must be gently shaken from side to side to indicate no further refill required. Failure to do so will result in the cup being continuousl topped up!

▼ *Whilst many of these buildings still stand, some have now been demolished to make space for more modern development. In the sixties Sheikh Rashid would often drive around the emirate unaccompanied and, when someone spotted him, word would be sent: "Raja aaya" – "the king has come" – and Ramesh would jump on to his bicycle to photograph Dubai through the eyes of the Sheikh. On occasion Sheikh Rashid would place stones at a certain site, marking out the positions of new buildings – Dubai Municipality, Etisalat, the Chamber of Commerce – rising out of the sand in his mind's eye.*

▲ The Emirtel Tower was the hub of
Dubai's telecommunications system in
1967. At its foot the dredging of the
Creek and associated land reclamation
was proceeding apace.

Taking an abra from the Municipality Library in Deira to Bur Dubai, two ladies and a young boy cross the creek. Beyond the bend of the water past the library is Dubai's first seat of learning, Al Madrassah Al Ahmadiya, known today as Umm Al Madares — Mother of Schools — built some 80 years ago by Sheikh Ahmed bin Dalmuk.

(Overleaf) Spectral in the morning mist, dhows and abras crowd the creek. So busy was the waterway in the late sixties that the journey across could sometimes be hazardous — on one occasion, Ramesh recalls, a fully loaded abra was run over by a dhow, throwing the luckless passengers into the water.

In Deira market birds and fish were sold — as they still are today. This large seagull found a comfortable if unconventional perch and, much to the child's delight, the moment was captured on film.

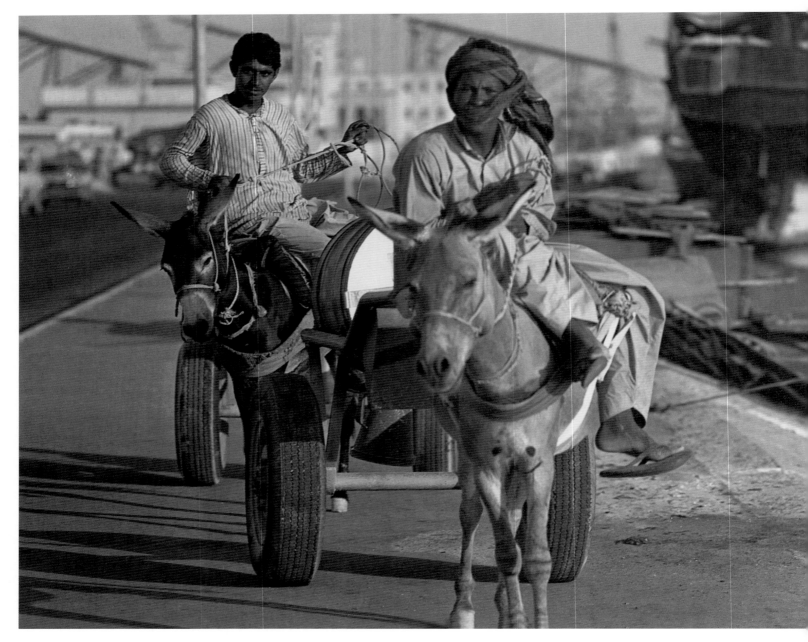

▲ *There was no running water in 1967 and throughout the day donkey carts would circulate around town, selling water for one anna per gallon. A single tin would hold four gallons and four of these made up a donkey-load. A family of four would use, typically, five tins a day and the water-vendors like these would do brisk business with twenty or thirty of them coming every day. In 1961 the average daily water supply to the city was 120,000 gallons; by 1975 this had increased to 8.75 million gallons.*

▶ *Carrying his umbrella in the bundle on his back, this elderly gentleman is standing opposite Sheikh Saeed's house in the curve of the road under which, just eight years later, the Shindaga tunnel would burrow its way to Al Ra on the other bank of the creek.*

▲ A group of men meet in Deira. One is sewing his kandoor with gold braid, others chat, whilst the gentleman in the foreground seems intrigued by the camera. The air, pungent with spices from the souq, is filled with the talk of buyers and sellers, the sounds and aromas creating an evocative atmosphere.

▶ On voyages of more than three days the ship's complement would normally include a cook — and often a double crew so that one shift could work whilst the other rested. The sailors lived a nomadic existence, rarely staying in one place for more than a week at a time.

▲ *Near the Ambassador Hotel and close to where the old General Post Office stood, a lime or nimboo seller takes a break from trading to puff on his pipe. Behind him the lady is selling tobacco leaves. The pace of life was still leisurely at this time.*

◀ *A camel owned by Sheikh Hamdan awaits the beginning of a race. Both male and female beasts participate in races from the age of four females retiring at around eight to ten years of age, whilst males often continue to compete until as old as fifteen. Traditionally, camel races were staged at any convenient location during weddings and other festive or social occasions, but nowadays there are also formal tracks and a programmed schedule of meetings.*

By now all the emirates were in the throes of change – but to greatly varying extent. Fujairah in 1968 was still not so very different from the village described by Lorimer in 1908: "150 houses of mud and stone, and a few of gypsum and cement, the entire village is surrounded by a nine foot high wall. There is plenty of water to be had from the wells and during the date harvest the people camp in 'barastis' among the plantations outside the village."

The seafarers of Ras Al Khaimah turned their attention to the agricultural development of their relatively fertile hinterland, the newly built highway linking the mountainous emirate with Dubai – just 75 kilometres away and providing a ready market for fresh produce.

In Sharjah, where the Trucial Coast's first trade school had opened in 1958 (instructing its 18 students in carpentry and vehicle maintenance), the number of pupils had now grown to 104 with an increased number of subjects. When the Trucial Oman Scouts decided to set up facilities for the training of personnel for skilled employment after their discharge, they located it in Sharjah because of the record already established by the older institution.

And in Dubai, where larger vessels still had to anchor offshore and have their goods brought to the customs wharf by abras, Sheikh Rashid sought to improve the situation by ordering construction of seven deep-water berths at the new Port Rashid. Capable of handling ships of up to 30' draught, the addition of these facilities marked the beginning of a period of meteoric growth in Dubai's economy.

◀ *Today this watchtower is overlooked by the Al Maqta'a Bridge, which links the island of Abu Dhabi to the mainland.*

A parade of camels at the Sharjah camel race – attended by Sheikh Zayed, Sheikh Rashid, and other dignitaries.

After a banquet following the race Sheikh Zayed and Sheikh Rashid share a joke.

Enjoying a sulaimani tea Sheikh Zayed listens as Sheikh Rashid converses with Sheikh Ahmed Al Thani of Qatar.

When the Sheikhs travelled in the ~~E~~mirates they were usually accompanied ~~by~~ a security guard – this one, in Sharjah, ~~ca~~rrying three guns and keeping a ~~w~~atchful eye on the activities of the ~~ph~~otographer. Having not encountered a ~~ca~~mera before he was puzzled, but made ~~no~~ objection.

(Overleaf) A lone boat rocks gently in the sea at sunset in front of the Corniche in Abu Dhabi. Shoals of sardines, anchovies and mackerel come close to shore and are caught in seine nets. In deeper water tuna, bonito, sailfish and kingfish are plentiful.

The earliest modern medical facilitie
in the region were a Protestant missio
that opened in Dubai in 1952 and
small obstetrical unit in Sharjah. The
inauguration of the Maktoum Hospita
marked the first fully-equipped hospital t
be opened in the area, offering treatmen
for virtually all types of illness. Her
families are waiting for treatment in th
hospital's large outpatients' clinic.

◀ Oil rigs at Fateh field, Dubai's first
offshore installation, were supplied and
serviced by barges based on the creek.

▼ The Dubai Municipality building i
1968 was where people, often wit
falcons on their arms, would come t
apply for trade licences, paying thei
dues in rupees – still the local currenc
at the time. The municipal counci
actively encouraged all forms of trade.

At the mouth of the creek fishermen bring in the day's catch whilst vendors wait to take the fresh fish to the market. The abra operator buys the fish from the dhows and, after the short journey to the shore, resells it to the vendors.

Early morning at Deira fish market. Fishing had always been a source of income and a favourite pastime — and provided a livelihood for fishermen who would go out in all weathers to provide residents with a constant, fresh supply, there being no adequate storage facilities for such a perishable commodity.

The word 'souq' conjures up images of narrow alleyways bustling with people and lined with shops – and many of Dubai's markets are just like that. The vegetable souq, however, provides a more open aspect – although the noise, calls of greeting and animated discussions between buyer and seller are much the same.

▲ *In Shindaga a badgeer — windtower — is surrounded by trees. Each tower is different in detail, some having two cavities on each side, others three or more, whilst the decorative curlicues in traditional Islamic style reflected the taste of the owners of the house — as well as the idiosyncrasies of the builder.*

Sheikh Mohammed bin Rashid Al Maktoum visits a school close to Nasser square. The children, part of a scout troop, form an impromptu guard of honour.

Just a handful of vehicles travelled along Abu Dhabi's Corniche in 1968 — although the buildings being constructed in the distance portend the enormous changes that were to come.

This elderly man and his donkey often rested in front of Ramesh's house around noon-time — and the old man welcomed the offer of a glass of water or sulaimani tea. Here he is pictured with a lady carrying a basket of grass on her head, probably for use as fodder.

Heralding the economic and social changes upon which the Emirates had embarked was a massive resettlement programme in the western region of Abu Dhabi. Sheikh Zayed saw the need for permanent homes for the nomadic Bedu and the new towns of Madinat Zayed, Ghaydia and Bida Al Mudawa were constructed to provide settled communities with schools, clinics and other modern amenities.

Dubai's rapid expansion had required the development of a range of additional services. Water resources at Aweer had been tapped to provide an increased supply to the city; during the first decade of its operation the Dubai Electricity Company had built four 33-kilowatt power stations and 68 sub-stations to reach its 10,723 consumers; and 1969 saw automatic traffic signals make their debut in the city – the rapid increase in population and the sharp rise in the number of vehicles causing concern about safety.

Dubai Petroleum Company had started developing the Fateh field and production, albeit on a limited scale, commenced on September 6 – the long-awaited export of oil becoming a reality when, on September 22, the first tanker took aboard 180,000 barrels. The unique arrangements for storing and loading Fateh's oil represented the successful application of an innovative concept that permitted offshore production operations to be conducted without the need for pipes to be laid to land. The khazzan storage system utilises two simple principles – oil and water do not mix, and oil is lighter than water. The khazzans themselves are huge structures the height of a fifteen-storey building and shaped like inverted glasses, which are sunk on the sea bed. As oil is pumped into the khazzan from the top, water is forced out from the bottom, leaving the tank full of oil. Conversely, as oil is drawn from the top of the khazzan to fill the waiting tanker, the sea-water level rises in the tank, forcing the floating oil upwards.

Oil was of course a welcome contributor to Dubai's economy, but trade continued to be of paramount importance to the emirate. In 1958 the city's imports were valued at £8 million. In 1967 the figure reached £42 million, in 1968 £70 million and in 1969 £81 million. Dubai, already an important port, was now establishing itself as the commercial centre of the Gulf.

Dubai's Clock Tower, built in the early 1960s, is still a focal point and familiar landmark – although now surrounded by high-rise buildings. Today's drivers in Dubai, despite the freeways and flyovers, must yearn for the empty roads enjoyed by their predecessors.

Ajman, the smallest of the seve[n] emirates with an area of just 78[?] square kilometres, has survived as a[n] independent entity for some 200 years[,] testimony to the wisdom of its Rule[rs] who successfully steered the tiny sta[te] through the political cross-currents an[d] shifting alliances that once typified th[e] region. But just to be on the safe si[de] they built this sturdy fort.

Related to the Ha'im of Al Ain, th[e] people of Ajman were probab[ly] originally attracted here by the sea[,] and fishing and dhow building sti[ll] flourish in the emirate.

The fort at Fujairah, renovated i[n] the sixties with unsympathet[ic] concrete, served as a look-out post an[d] place of refuge. The east coast was on[e] of the last areas to benefit from th[e] wealth derived from oil and – becau[se] of its later development – has ma[ny] historical buildings which still rema[in] largely intact.

Abundant sweet water in the area around Khat in Ras Al Khaimah supports a wide variety of trees including neem (melia azedarach), peepul (ficus religiosa) and the date palm (phoenix dactylifera). Khat is also known for its hot springs — the sulphur-rich water, welling into pools at a comfortable 35°C, being believed to have medicinal properties. Certainly the Portuguese thought so — they were frequent visitors to the springs towards the end of the last century — and in more recent times the waters are purported to have cured skin ailments.

A Bedu leads his goat along Bani Yas Street in Deira – the animal in all probability destined to be the main course in the next family meal.

▲ *Recently off-loaded from a dhow, a herd of cattle is escorted through Nasser square. Cows, goats and other livestock were frequent passengers on the dhows that plied between Dubai and the subcontinent.*

▲ Camels walking along the bank of
the creek are overtaken by a hurrying
donkey pulling an oil drum full of
kerosene. Before electricity was readily
available many households were lit by
kerosene lanterns.

▶ Through the openings in a plywood
cabin in front of the Ruler's Office on the
Dubai side of the creek, two ladies can be
seen being carefully rowed across.

▲ A windtower rises into the skyline above decorated parapet walls made from precast concrete panels, the regularity of the machine-made patterns in contrast with the individual features of design in traditional architecture. It is in this very house that Ramesh set up his art gallery in 1993.

▲ Soaring columns, shapely arches and decorative plaster work adorn this pre-1960's balcony. Most of the old buildings were made from coral stone, limestone and timber, but as the city developed and modern materials became available the traditional methods fell out of use.

This splendid house, once the residence of the Kuwaiti ambassador, still stands, now facing the Sheraton Hotel. However, land reclamation has altered its desirable creek-side position — it is now located a few hundred metres inland.

▲ *This view of Maktoum Street shows few buildings – but an early example of the determination to make the city attractive can be seen in the planted central reservation between the two carriageways. A great deal of work is in progress on the creek front and, in the distance, the Clock Tower and the now six-year-old Maktoum Bridge can just be discerned.*

The khazzans – the word being Arabic for storage – were built by the
Chicago Bridge and Iron Company, whose huge construction works
dominated this section of Jumeirah beach – which is how the seemingly
oddly-named Chicago Beach area acquired its title.

▲ Behind the windtowers of Bastakia the new skyline of Dubai is emerging. The cars parked outside the Ruler's office have taken advantage of man-made protection from the sun, abandoning the natural shade provided by the tree.

▶ A fisherman carries a good-sized pair of hammour to the fish market at Al Ras – where fresh fish is still sold today. Fish provided an essential source of protein for the people of the Emirates. Whilst fishing goes on all year, the period from September to March is the busiest and most productive since at this time the colder, less saline water from the Indian Ocean flows strongly into the Gulf, bringing with it sardines, mackerel, tuna and other fish. Using purse-seine nets which are dropped vertically and closed with a pull of the string-like pouch, the UAE fisherman reaps a rich harvest indeed.

▲ *The young Sheikh Ahmed bin Saeed Al Maktoum, now Chairman of Emirates and President of Dubai Department of Civil Aviation, sits with Sheikh Rashid as he receives Eid greetings.*

▲ A group of folk singers and dancers gathers outside a barasti house in Satwa. Traditional Bedu song and dance was much influenced by the music of Zanzibar, off the East African coast, with which the people of the Emirates had long been trading. Dances are performed with great energy and grace, the rhythm being supplied by the beating of drums and the clashing of cymbals.

The drums would probably have been made from goatskin. The large instrument in the centre – looking like a cross between a harp and a guitar – is a tamboura.

The seven emirates that would come to form the UAE – although sharing the same faith and cultural background – were remarkably diverse. Disparate in geographical size and wealth, each owed allegiance to a different Ruler and all had a long history of rivalry. Curiously it was this fierce loyalty that enabled the formation of the UAE, for once the Rulers themselves agreed, their peoples were happy to follow.

As preparations continued for the formation of the new country, economic, social and structural development proceeded apace. In Dubai the Government created the Department of Health and Medical Services which took over the running of the Maktoum Hospital from the Municipality and set about organising the further expansion of medical facilities. And in November Dubai's rapidly growing economy was given further impetus by the discovery of a second offshore field some 16 kilometres south-west of Fateh.

During this period the re-export of gold continued to play a major role in Dubai's commercial sector. In the first half of the century Kuwait had been the leading player in the trade, but the growth in Kuwait's oil revenues in the 1950s opened up other opportunities for the country's merchants and the gold trade moved to Dubai. Gold was bought in Europe and imported duty-free to Dubai, where it was sold to syndicates of merchants who would re-export it to India and Pakistan. The turnover in the gold business increased steadily, reaching a record 259 tonnes in 1970, when Dubai carried the distinction of being the world's third largest buyer of gold on the open market.

Sultan Qaboos bin Said took over the reins of power in Oman in July 1970. His citizens greeted his accession positively, anticipating correctly that under his leadership the country would emerge from its near-medieval past and join the march of progress already so well established in Dubai. Here Sheikh Maktoum congratulates His Majesty.

Sheikh Maktoum (centre) and Sheikh Khalifa bin Zayed Al Nahyan (left), Crown Prince of Abu Dhabi, in conversation during the celebrations in Muscat marking the accession of Sultan Qaboos bin Said to the Omani throne.

▲ *Probably originally constructed around 1760, the handsome Diwan Amiri or Manhar Palace in Abu Dhabi has been much extended over the centuries. The building was the traditional residence of the emirate's Rulers and it was here, in a small building by the main gate, that the historic agreement that created the United Arab Emirates was signed. For several years it was the meeting place of the Federal National Council before being adapted to its current role as the Documentation Centre for Historical Research.*

Sheikh Maktoum arrives for his wedding, accompanied by his younger brother, Sheikh Ahmed bin Rashid, on the left.

▲ *Sheikh Khalid bin Mohammed Al Qassimi, Ruler of Sharjah, Sheikh Rashid and Sheikh Zayed enjoy a jovial moment during the celebrations.*

▲ *Also celebrating the marriage of Sheikh Maktoum, these gentlemen are performing a Nubian dance sequence believed to have the power to heal and to drive out evil spirits through the chanting of verses and the beating of drums.*

▶ *Sheikh Zayed in the midst of th* *crowd celebrating the marriage, i* *1970, of Sheikh Maktoum, the preser* *Ruler of Dubai. The traditional danc* *being performed to the accompanimer* *of large tambourine-like drums is th* *ardha.*

The server of gahwa passes amongst guests that comprise members of the diplomatic corps, dignitaries and prominent businessmen — including Majid Al Futtaim, seen here second from the right.

Citizens, accompanied by the playing and singing of musicians, are celebrating the wedding of Sheikh Maktoum. The small earthenware bucket contains embers which were used to warm the skins of the tambourines and keep them taut.

After prayers at Eid, Sheikh Rashid would take time from his official engagements to visit his close friend Jamai'a Al Basti before returning to Zabeel Palace to receive guests.

▲ *Taken from the roof of a building overlooking Nasser square, this photograph dramatically records the area's development and progress. In the background the sea is full of ships waiting to unload, whilst the square is dominated by two of the tallest buildings in town – the British Bank of the Middle East on the left hand side of the picture and the twelve storeys of the Phoenicia Hotel – foretelling the changes yet to come.*

▲ *Man and bird share the same keen eye. Falconry has been practised in the Emirates for hundreds of years by both sheikhs and ordinary folk. The skill of the falconer is tested when he takes his charge out into the desert and releases the falcon to chase its prey – its return dependent on how well it has been trained.*

▼ *Visitors from other Arab countries would often attend camel races in Dubai, Sharjah and Abu Dhabi. Here a group of Omani buyers examines the beasts before a race. Nature designed the camel's hoof so that it does not slip in even the finest sand – and one leading tyre company is said to have studied this phenomenon when designing tyres for use in the desert.*

▲ *Close to where the Hyatt Regency now stands a huge crowd gathered as the news spread of the death of Gamal Abdul Nasser at the age of 52. During his tenure as President of Egypt educational facilities had been greatly developed and, by the seventies, the country was providing teachers, engineers, doctors, pharmacists and administrators to fulfil the increasing needs of other Arab nations, including the Emirates.*

▲ *UAE citizens and expatriates make their way along Bani Yas Street in mourning of the death of Gamal Abdul Nasser.*

The years of planning culminated on December 2, 1971, when the United Arab Emirates was formed by the signing of the provisional constitution. Whilst not intended immediately to bind the different emirates into a completely uniform community, it provided a framework within which, over time, this could be achieved. The political structure agreed by the Rulers was grafted onto the traditional local governments, allowing continuity of administration whilst a federal system was developed.

The constitution gives responsibility for general policy decisions to the Supreme Council. Executive authority lies with the Council of Ministers, headed by the Prime Minister and collectively accountable to the Supreme Council. The Cabinet – in which all the emirates are given representation – is charged with the task of initiating legislation. The people's participation is ensured by the country's parliament, the Federal National Council, whose members act as a watchdog over the implementation of approved projects. FNC members are appointed by the Rulers according to a quota agreed in the constitution.

The year saw progress in many other fields too. Dubai's international airport came into operation in May, the design of its attractive terminal building and control tower being inspired by traditional architectural styles; Al Ain's excellent museum was opened, presenting a splendid collection of ethnic items including clothes, gold and silver jewellery, horse and camel saddles, weapons, tools, household items and artefacts from the archaeological digs at Al Ain and Umm Al Nar; and excavations in Dubai also revealed evidence that the region had before been home to a sophisticated urban civilisation.

◄ *As the independence agreement is signed by Sheikh Zayed on December 2, 1971 a nation is born. Political pundits of the time were sceptical about the future of the federation, some even predicting its disintegration within the first year. Happily they were wrong and the UAE has not merely survived but prospered.*

▲ *Sheikh Rashid sits by Sheikh Zayed's side as the agreement is signed in Abu Dhabi. He is accompanied by his sons Sheikh Maktoum, the Crown Prince, Sheikh Hamdan and Sheikh Mohammed.*

A historic moment under the new flag – from left to right Sheikh Maktoum bin Rashid Al Maktoum, Crown Prince of Dubai; Sheikh Khalid bin Mohammed Al Qassimi, Ruler of Sharjah; Sheikh Rashid bin Saeed Al Maktoum, Ruler of Dubai; Sheikh Zayed bin Sultan Al Nahyan, Ruler of Abu Dhabi; Sheikh Rashid bin Humaid Al Nuaimi, Ruler of Ajman; Sheikh Mohammed bin Hamad Al Sharqi, Ruler of Fujairah; and Sheikh Rashid bin Ahmed Al Mualla, Crown Prince of Umm Al Quwain. Although attending the meeting Sheikh Saqr bin Mohammed Al Qassimi, Ruler of Ras Al Khaimah, did not sign the agreement at this time and it was not until February of the following year that the emirate joined the federation.

▲ *Reflections in Nasser square. A new mosque is rising above a row of small shops now long since demolished.*

▶ *Portrait of an old man well wrapped up against the winter wind.*

▲ *Nasser square, before the car took over, was the venue for the livestock market where dozens of vendors and their families worked in an atmosphere of bonhomie and camaraderie. The little chap in the centre of the picture under the umbrella attracts immediate attention with his frog hat.*

▶ *An abra boatman takes a break fro undertaking repairs. Originally abr passengers would have to scramble ashor on the sandy banks of the creek bu nowadays there are specially bui landing points.*

▲ *Shindaga market was popular with shoppers – even when heavy rain flooded the area. Here they would come to inspect limes, dates, sugar-cane, vegetables, goats, cows and camels – and to animatedly discuss prices.*

Al Fahidi Fort, considered to be the oldest building in the city, was constructed some 200 years ago, initially to protect the town and provide refuge. In subsequent years it became variously the seat of government, an arms and ammunition store and the central jail. Now it was to begin a more peaceful phase as a museum and, enjoying refreshments amongst the abras and shashis, are some of those who attended the inauguration.

The occasion is the opening by Sheikh Rashid of the Dubai Museum in May. Ramesh recalls that he asked the Ruler to pose for a photograph by the cannon. At first he refused – but then suddenly walked up the steps to the ramparts leaving the other invitees in the courtyard below. To be alone with Sheikh Rashid even for a few moments was, says Ramesh, a privilege accorded to few.

It was part of Sheikh Rashid's routine to spend an hour or so in his office at the beginning of the day. Ramesh was occasionally allowed in quietly to photograph the Ruler at work.

Sheikh Rashid at the newly opened Dubai International Airport. The new airport was able to cope with the sudden spurt of passengers flying into Dubai and the increasing frequency of airline services.

The seventies, a decade which in many other parts of the world was marked by the twin ogres of recession and inflation, was a period of spectacular development in the United Arab Emirates, where annual growth rates between 1972 and 1980 averaged a staggering 40.5%.

At independence federation had been little more than a concept and the provisional constitution merely a document that outlined what might be done. But the close co-operation between the members of the Supreme Council – the Rulers of each emirate – who surrendered many of their individual rights and powers to the Federal Government ensured that the progress towards true federalisation moved ahead rapidly. A Supreme Court was created, having jurisdiction over disputes between member emirates as well as between any one of them and the federation; a federal passport was introduced, replacing those issued individually by each emirate, their holders becoming citizens of the UAE; stamps were issued nationwide. In these and dozens of other ways both the fact and the idea of federation were promoted.

In Abu Dhabi pioneering work was being carried out to reduce the nation's dependence on imported foodstuffs. In Al Ain and the Western Region dry-land farming techniques were changing the landscape, whilst at Sadiyat Island near Abu Dhabi large-scale hydroponic farming was taking place: here, under vast plastic roofs, the seeds of tomato, pepper, cucumber and other vegetables were sown directly into sand, their roots being fed water and fertilisers by drip irrigation.

In Dubai, helped by the rapid development of port and airport facilities, the effort remained concentrated on trade – which would lead to a 600% increase in the value of imports between 1973 and 1977.

Lady reading. Abu Dhabi had three local ladies at its radio and television stations who would read the news, organise children's variety programmes and sometimes act in plays. Unusually for those times the Ministry of the Interior also employed ladies, mainly to deal with female travellers at the airport – and to attend to women under arrest – and the Abu Dhabi Police had started a recruitment drive to attract women into the force.

(Previous page) The occasion of the UAE's first National Day attracted crowds of all nationalities to the Abu Dhabi corniche, joining the Ruler and other dignitaries. The lady wearing her burqa and dressed in fustan with a young child in her arms symbolised to Ramesh the birth of the nation.

Men, women and children turned out in large numbers to watch the first National Day celebrations in Abu Dhabi on December 2, 1972. Such events helped to foster a sense of national identity — although the young lady in her mother's arms seems to have been overcome by the excitement and is taking a nap.

During a visit to Sharjah, Sheikh Zayed enjoys a meal as the guest of Sheikh Sultan bin Mohammed Al Qassimi of Sharjah.

▲ *Sheikh Zayed receives the Sudanese President Jaafar Nimeiry who arrived in Fujairah by sea. Greeted by a large crowd – and some well-armed security personnel – the two Presidents met to discuss the proposed investment by the UAE in developing uncultivated land in the Sudan.*

◀ *Nowadays one has to search for the ...d Diwan Amiri amongst Abu Dhabi's ...wering office blocks and it is hard to ...nagine how it once dominated the town. ...onstructed from rocks and mortared ...ith mud, the structure was surprisingly ...rong – and today is a pleasing link with ...e city's past. This unusual photograph ...as taken from the interior of what is ...ow the Documentation Centre for ...istorical Research.*

▲ *The growth from small town to modern metropolis takes generations in most parts of the world – but in Abu Dhabi the transformation has been accomplished in just twenty years. The effort to bring twentieth-century amenities to the population has not been restricted to the city – throughout the Emirates houses have been constructed by the Government and given rent free to poorer families.*

▲ *Bank Saderat Iran's smart new offices on Dubai's Maktoum Street had few neighbours in 1972. On the left the Deira Cinema can be seen in the distance, whilst on the right is the original Emirtel Tower (now Etisalat) and the old Municipality building. One of the city's first restaurants opened near here, where diners could enjoy Lebanese cuisine either indoors or alfresco in a walled courtyard. Later the old Carlton Tower Hotel opened, where guests would dance the night away before settling down to a gigantic breakfast.*

▼*The completion of Port Rashid in 1972 – eighteen months ahead of schedule – was marked by an opening ceremony that attracted a large crowd to see Sheikh Mohammed officially inaugurate the new facility. The project, at the time, was often described as ambitious – a euphemism for unnecessary – but as was invariably the case Sheikh Rashid's judgement proved to be correct and the new port made, and still makes, a significant contribution to Dubai's ability to trade.*

▲ *Sheikh Rashid was a regular visitor to the offices of Dubai Municipality, where he maintained a sparsely furnished office. An adjacent meeting room was transferred into an impromptu gallery when Sheikh Hamdan, having seen some of Ramesh's photographs, asked him to mount a display. This, Ramesh's first exhibition, resulted in Sheikh Hamdan purchasing copies of every single picture.*

Sheikh Rashid in conversation with Easa Saleh Al Gurg, later to become the UAE's Ambassador to Britain, at the opening of an Indian exhibition at Dubai International Airport. Events were often staged in the airport's arrivals lounge, then one of the few buildings large enough to accommodate such displays. On the left of the picture is the Indian Ambassador, Mr S E H Rizvi.

▲ *An interesting variety of boats moored at Deira, with Bur Dubai and the Ruler's Office on the other side of the creek. For a century Deira had been ruled independently of Dubai and it was not until the 1950s that the two towns were united.*

▲ *It is just after dawn and the abras are still moored, not yet needed for the commuter rush. Behind them a large boum can be seen slipping past the minaret of a mosque before heading out to the open sea.*

The process of integrating the formerly independent emirates into a federal whole accelerated during 1973. The Currency Board was one of the most important of the new federal institutions, assuming the responsibilities of the central bank and regulating monetary and banking affairs. Before federation different monies were used but, on May 19, the dirham, now one of the world's most stable currencies, was introduced nationwide.

Another major step was the setting up of a National Planning Board. Hitherto each emirate had been developing within its own area, without reference to or consultation with the others, often leading to duplication of development projects. The new board provided a forum which enabled the integration of projects on a national level.

The federal Ministry of Information and Culture was also established in 1973, empowered to codify press law, assume responsibility for the running of radio and television stations and regulate the import of publications.

Improvement in health care was high on the agenda in 1973. Although Dubai had opened the first well-equipped hospital in the region during the 1950s, the inauguration of the Rashid Hospital in early 1973 marked a huge improvement in medical facilities. Initially a 400-bed complex with medical, surgical, obstetric, orthopaedic and intensive care departments, it was soon expanded to include geriatric and physiotherapy units.

And rapid progress was made in the educational field by the introduction of a unified school curriculum, designed to create equal opportunities across the country as well as foster the concept of nationhood in the new generation.

Dubai also featured on the world scene through less fortunate occurrences. On July 20 a Japan Airlines Boeing 747 was hijacked and forced to land at Dubai. For the three days and nights that it remained stranded Defence Minister Sheikh Mohammed led the teams of negotiators round-the-clock, before the aircraft eventually left for Damascus with hijackers and passengers. Barely four months later Sheikh Mohammed was once again called to the airport – this time to deal with the hijackers of a KLM jumbo with 247 passengers on board. It left soon afterwards for Aden, but returned to Dubai when refused permission to land. Prolonged negotiations followed which resulted in the hijackers' surrender.

The mountains of Dibba on the east coast were not easy to reach until linked by modern highways. Here, in a wadi, a Bedouin lady has collected water from the village well and is transporting it home. Dibba was famed in the ancient world – its praises were sung in the Caliph's court at Baghdad by the poet Abu Bakr bin Dhuaraid of Khatt, who told of a city whose riches were beyond compare. Dibba is also the site of a battle, fought in 633 AD, which marked the final stage of the Muslim conquest of the Arabian peninsula.

▲ A young Bedouin camel jockey gazes over the neck of his mount. Camel racing is an exciting sport enjoyed by UAE citizens and expatriates alike – although Ramesh advises care since being hit by the hoof of a camel whilst attempting to take a photograph during a race.

Wooden fishing boats anchor in the calm waters of Khorfakkan Bay, where the Hajar Mountains sweep down to the palm groves that line the water's edge. Further south lie the mangrove forests at Khor Kalba, home to the white-collared kingfisher, a bird unique to the UAE and Oman.

Khorfakkan – one of Sharjah's three enclaves on the UAE's scenic east coast – attracts not only trading ships but holidaymakers too. The rocky coastline shelters secluded sandy bays and, offshore, easily accessible coral reefs.

▲ *The rooftops of Bur Dubai, near the Ambassador Hotel, were, in 1973, a mixture of old and new. In the distance, on the other side of the creek, the first of Deira's multi-storey buildings are harbingers of the dramatic changes yet to come.*

▲ *Sheikh Rashid and his son Sheikh Mohammed lead the Eid prayers.*

▶ *(Overleaf) Just part of the huge congregation that assembled for Eid prayers at Eid Mussallah near Port Rashid. Throughout the Muslim world the two most important festivals are Eid al Fitr and Eid al Adha – and their celebration is an integral part of the lives of the people.*

▲ *Where the shops of Jashanmal & Sons and Alfulaij & Company
used to stand is now Nasser square. The Jashanmals set up this store
in 1956 when the elder brother, Atma, came to Dubai from Bahrain.
The shop was a focal point for residents who wished to buy clothing,
perfumes, books and magazines.*

▲The smallest supermarket in the world? The lady is selling an assortment of goods, from which Ramesh purchased eight annas' worth after taking her photograph. Today the Shindaga tunnel runs underneath this spot.

1974

Throughout the country the continued development demanded additional resources – from power supplies to education, airports to engineers. In Dubai, where the demand for power had increased by 35% during the decade, installation of new, large power plants became a necessity – work commencing on the first gas-turbine station in 1974.

Dubai Airport's efficient services won international recognition when it was chosen as the stopover for the Far East test flights of Concorde – although increased fuel costs and difficulties in obtaining overflying rights from other countries led to the service later being abandoned.

The number of girls' schools had reached twenty by 1974, reflecting the importance society was attaching to female education.

In February the UAE established its initial par value with the International Monetary Fund, the dirham being valued at 0.186621 grams of fine gold. And gold, although not traded on the huge scale of the 1960s, continued to be an important part of the economy, the souq being crowded with local ladies in search of marriyahs – heavy necklaces; fataka – toe-rings; and abugaden – large earrings. Europeans were looking for delicate, finely-worked pieces in 18-carat, Iranians sought 21-carat stone-studded items and Indians and Pakistanis searched for 22-carat jewellery. Dubai, of course, had plentiful supplies of all.

◀ *Not all the shopping was for gold. In the vegetable market radish, coriander, spinach, fenugreek, tobacco leaves, dates, garlic and dozens of other vegetables are piled in aromatic profusion, providing buyers and sellers an opportunity to exchange news and gossip.*

▲ The British Bank of the Middle East lost not only its monopoly but its position as the bankers to the government when, by Emiri decree, the National Bank of Dubai was set up in 1963. This locally incorporated bank was authorised by the government to represent the Qatar-Dubai Currency Board and issue as well as redeem its currency.

Soon international banks, realising the potential, were establishing a presence in Dubai. First National City Bank – having secured rights from the US Treasury to deal in gold – set up their office on a prime location by the creek.

The seafaring tradition is strong throughout the Gulf and shipping forms an important part of the economy. This is the old port at Abu Dhabi, pictured before the beginning of its major development as the newly named Mina Zayed.

The view from Eastern Bank's offices overlooking the creek in Bur Dubai must have made it a pleasant place to work. The ease with which the UAE switched from the Bahraini dinar and Qatar-Dubai riyal to the dirham was an extraordinary feat, requiring the exchange of some 260 million dirhams in just six months. The efficiency with which the operation was conducted impressed the international banking community and greatly increased confidence in the fledgling state's banking sector. Within a year of the establishment of the Currency Board the UAE had seen seven locally incorporated and nineteen foreign banks open.

The long, low building is the General Post Office and the trucks parked on the sand beside it are Bedfords, ubiquitous in the Emirates at the time having been left behind by the departing British forces. Even today, a few of these sturdy vehicles may still be seen smokily plying the roads of the UAE.

▲Camel racing dates back to ancient times when contests were organised to test the strength of animals. A good trainer is an expert on the behaviour and moods of his animal – as well as being versed in preparing them for races by careful supervision of their diet and by walking them over long distances to improve stamina and performance.

▲ *Arabs have been keen falconers for centuries, although the hunt nowadays is purely for sport. The trainer of falcons is known as a saggar and, rarely separated from his bird, a strong bond of trust is established. The training takes between two and four weeks and only then is the bird allowed to hunt, the most likely prey being the hubara (MacQueen's Bustard), the stone curlew or perhaps an occasional hare.*

Great emphasis was now being placed on social matters – and especially so for women. The UAE Women's Association, under the active patronage of Sheikha Fatima, wife of the President, opened new branches in Dubai, Sharjah, Ajman and Umm Al Quwain during 1975. Each society had an executive committee dealing with religion, social affairs, culture, health, fine arts, public relations and nursery schools. Social workers at the centres made frequent visits to outlying communities, often accompanied by medical teams who undertook maternity checks, treated the young and educated the villagers in matters of general health and hygiene.

Educational programmes ensured that women – even those who had missed school in their youth – had the opportunity to learn how to read and write and to care better for their children. More than 1,000 women enrolled in the first stage of the adult literacy programme in 1972 – but with increasing literacy rates their numbers dwindled to less than 800 in 1975. Whether married or single the women attended regularly and absenteeism was low, reflecting the traditional respect for learning.

Preservation, important in such a rapidly changing place, was also brought into the agenda. A United Nations report on the preservation of cultural monuments identified Bastakia as a site of major importance, but throughout the seventies the future of this unique area hung in the balance as the requirement for development land increased. Thankfully, much of Bastakia remains for future generations to appreciate their heritage.

In Dubai a new financial institution that combined modern banking techniques with the tenets of Islam was launched. The Dubai Islamic Bank rapidly gained both recognition and success and has now become a major player in the financial sector.

◀ *This popular dance in which brightly attired girls swirl their flowing tresses of long hair is called naiashti. At one time no marriage ceremony would have been complete without the dance, but changing attitudes have diminished its popularity and, in public at least, the colourful, rhythmic naiashti is now only infrequently seen.*

▲ *Sheikh Hasher Al Maktoum photographed with one of his favourite falcons. Of the two birds most used in the UAE – the hurr and the shaheen – the latter is more popular because of its swiftness and perseverance in chasing its prey.*

The training of a bird can only be accomplished by the subtle imposition of the trainer's will through alternate fasting and feeding, the tethered falcon being offered lures at slowly increasing distances.

▶ *Proudly flying the UAE flag, this boat owned by Sheikh Maktoum is about to participate in a race on Dubai's creek.*

▶ *En route to Fujairah the road passes through the Hajar mountains, a remote region where the jagged peaks reach heights of 3,000 metres. Inhospitable though they may appear, enclosed in the steep-sided wadis are pockets of cultivation, green even at the height of summer.*

▲ *Sharjah, the third largest emirate, encompasses some 2,600 square kilometres and is unique in that it possesses territories that border both the Gulf and Indian Ocean coasts. Al Wahda Street is typical of the development that was being undertaken throughout the Emirates in the mid-seventies.*

▲ *A link with the past. Modern buildings now surround Bastakia's narrow alleyways. All healthy societies have to balance the pragmatic requirements of the future with the emotional need to retain some links with the past – but few have had to compress that process into such a short space of time. It is nice to know that the infant in the arms of the lady walking through the Bastakia of 1975 will have grown up in a city that, despite having changed so fast, enables him to trace his heritage back through the sandy paths of Bastakia to the lapping waters of the creek.*

Ramesh Shukla

Ramesh Shukla was born in India's Gujarat state in 1938, the son of a self-taught textile designer. He grew up in a traditional environment in which it was customary for the son to go into the family business, but the young man's life was to be dramatically changed by his father's present on his fourteenth birthday – a Rolleicord camera. All of Ramesh's early photographic work was done with this camera and although no longer working it is still one of his most treasured possessions.

Ramesh's photographic skills soon attracted national attention and in 1955 he was asked to undertake freelance commissions for *The Times of India*, the country's most prestigious English-language newspaper. During the next ten years he travelled extensively on assignments throughout the country.

He was invited to visit Dubai in 1965 and during that first two-month stay took pictures that are now some of the most important in his collection. After several further visits he returned to live in 1967 and set up his studio near Nasser square.

In 1968 he started taking photographs of the Rulers of the Emirates and in later years painted dozens of portraits. His photographs of the Rulers now adorn government buildings, palaces and private collections around the world. His picture of Sheikh Rashid appears on a postage stamp; that of a mosque may be seen on the 500 dirham note; and his picture of a falcon is carried on the UAE military uniform.

He has twice been invited to Oman on assignment for Sultan Qaboos, was the Royal Photographer during the visit of Queen Elizabeth II of Britain to the UAE in 1979, and accompanied Sheikh Mohammed to record a hunting tour. Ramesh has held a number of photographic exhibitions including special events for the Dubai Chamber of Commerce and Industry, the Saudi Arabian Ministry of Information, the United Kingdom's International Racing Bureau, and, in China, a display of his work on Arab life and culture at the request of the Chinese Government. In 1992 his exhibition 'Zayed in Pictures', held at the Abu Dhabi Cultural Foundation to mark the 26th anniversary of Sheikh Zayed's accession, achieved public acclaim and Ramesh was presented with a gold plate from the President in recognition of his work.

Largely self-taught, Ramesh says he has been much influenced and inspired by the works of the great photojournalists of the 1950s and '60s, and particularly by *Life* magazine. He lives in Dubai and his gallery, located in one of the windtower houses of his beloved Bastakia, contains a comprehensive selection of his photographs and paintings as well as the work of other artists. He is married with one son, a graduate of the University of Miami.

◄ *The young Ramesh, his wife Taru and son Neel at the edge of the creek. Neel and many other children would cross the waterway by abra to attend Our Own English School in Bur Dubai, a journey which occasionally ended, in the hurry of disembarkation, with an unscheduled swim. Then, as now, families would often engage an abra for an exclusive Friday cruise along the creek.*